W9-AQN-494

STAY HEALTHY

with Sesame Street

Understanding Coronavirus

Mary Lindeen

Lerner Publications ◆ Minneapolis

Health and hygiene are a key part of Sesame Workshop's mission to help kids grow smarter, stronger, and kinder. Elmo, Cookie Monster, and other furry friends from *Sesame Street* can help children understand what coronavirus is, what it looks like, and what happens when people get sick as well as how to stay healthy and connected. Understanding and preventing coronavirus can be as easy as ABC.

—Sincerely, the Editors at Sesame Workshop

TABLE OF CONTENTS

Let's Learn Together!

Elmo and his friends have been hearing a lot about coronavirus. Maybe you have questions about it. Your friends from Sesame Street are here to help you learn more.

Elmo has a lot of questions about coronavirus. Let's get some answers—together!

Coronavirus Questions and Answers

What is coronavirus?

Coronavirus is one type of virus. A virus is a germ that can get in our bodies and make us sick.

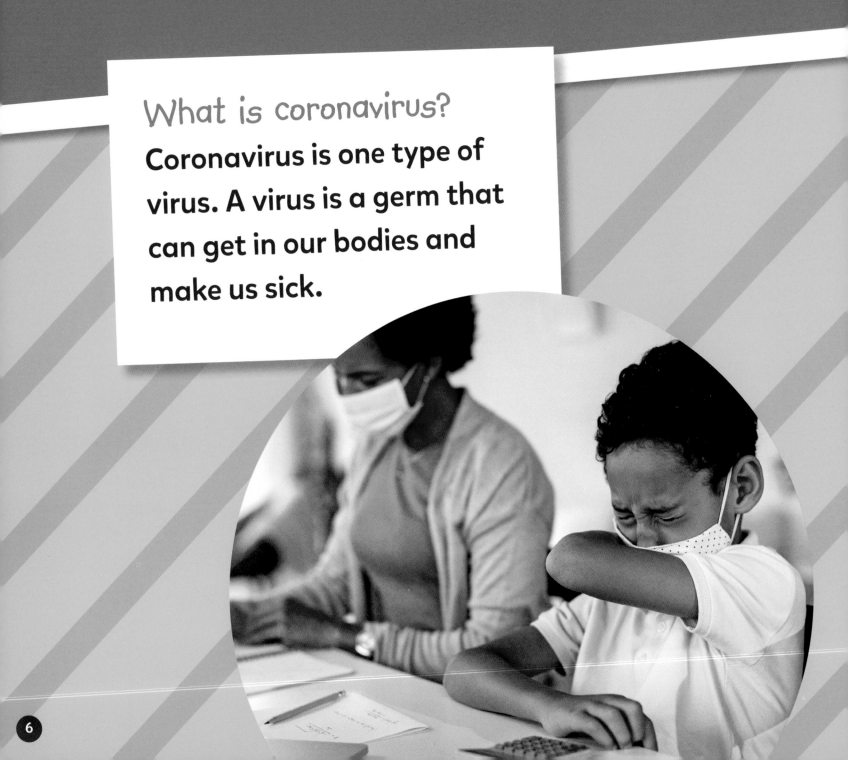

7

What does coronavirus look like?

Viruses are super tiny! They are so tiny that we can't see them with only our eyes. We need to look through a microscope.

Why are people talking about coronavirus?

People are talking about coronavirus because it can make them sick. No one likes to be sick.

11

What happens if you catch coronavirus?

Some people get sick from coronavirus. Some people don't feel sick at all. Doctors and nurses take care of us and help us to feel better.

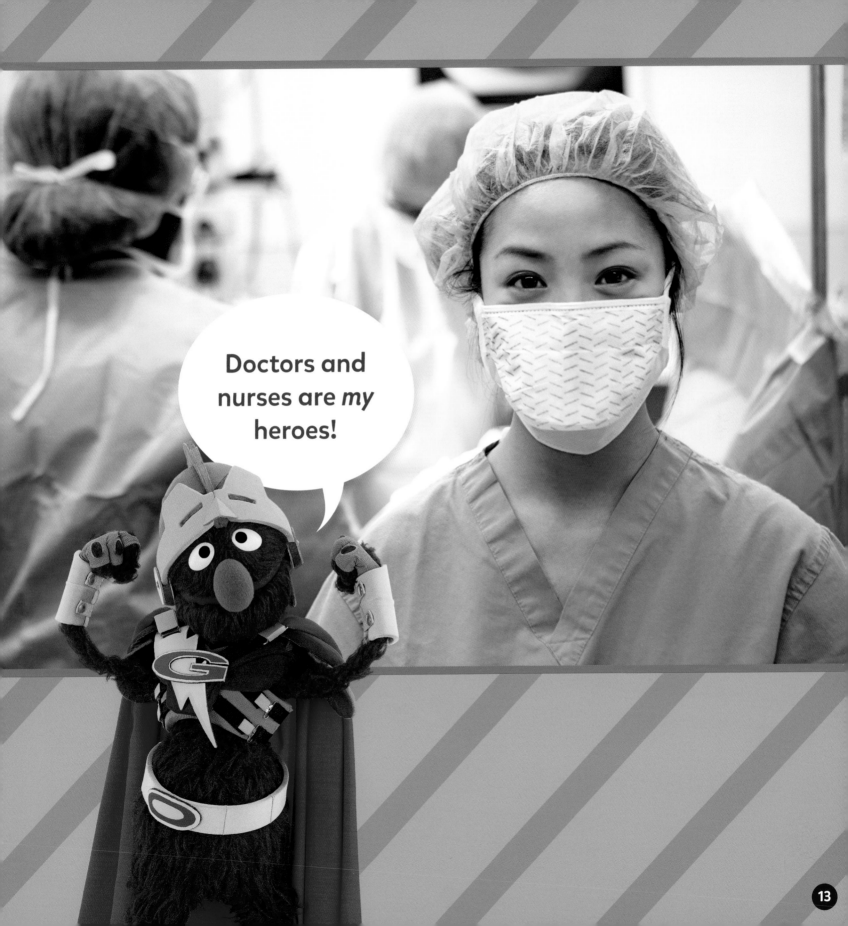

Who is helping with coronavirus?

Many people are helpers. Doctors and nurses are helping by taking care of sick people. Scientists are helping by creating medicine to help people feel better. Helpers are heroes!

Who else is helping?

Everyday heroes are helping too! Grocery store workers, delivery people, mail carriers, and bus drivers are helping. You can thank helpers by drawing them a picture!

How can we stay healthy?

We can take good care of our bodies. We can eat healthy foods, exercise, and get lots of sleep. Wash your hands often with soap and water.

How can we help our friends and family stay healthy?

You can wear a mask when you leave home. Cough and sneeze into your elbow. Wave hello to friends from a distance.

How can you *see* and play with friends and family when you are apart?

You can talk on the phone, have a video playdate, draw a picture, or send them a letter!

23

Changes Can Be Hard

Cookie Monster can't play outside today, and that makes him feel frustrated. Do you sometimes feel frustrated too?

Put your hands on your belly. Breathe in slowly through your nose and out slowly through your mouth. Cookie feels calmer! Do you?

Me like me belly and me like breathing. It good combination.

Staying home can be fun!

You might read a book or do a puzzle. Play a game. Have a dance party!

Build a pillow fort, or go on a scavenger hunt inside!

I love playing at home with my *mami*, my *papi*, and my *abuela*!

You're the Expert!

Experts are helping with coronavirus. You are an expert too! You know all about yourself. See if you can answer these questions about you!

What are your favorite games to play at home?

How can you keep your body healthy today?

Who do you like to video chat with?

What do you like best about staying home?

How can you thank a helper?

Glossary

distance: an amount of space between people, places, or things

frustrated: the feeling when you try to do something but can't

germ: a very tiny thing that makes a person sick when it gets inside the body

medicine: something that makes sick people better

virus: one kind of germ that makes people sick

Learn More

Hansen, Grace. *The COVID-19 Virus*. Minneapolis: Abdo Kids, 2020.

Kenney, Karen Latchana. *Calm Monsters, Kind Monsters: A Sesame Street Guide to Mindfulness*. Minneapolis: Lerner Publications, 2021.

Schuh, Mari. *Taking Care of Me: Healthy Habits with Sesame Street*. Minneapolis: Lerner Publications, 2021

Sesame Street: Caring for Each Other
https://www.sesamestreet.org/caring

Index

Photo Acknowledgments

Image credits: imtmphoto/Shutterstock.com, p. 4; LightField Studios/Shutterstock.com, p. 5; Drazen Zigic/iStock/Getty Images, p. 6; : GUNDAM_Ai/Studio/Shutterstock.com, p. 7; Prostock-studio/Shutterstock.com, p. 8; fizkes/Shutterstock.com, p. 9; Centers for Disease Control and Prevention Public Health Image Library/Alissa Eckert, MSMI; Dan Higgins, MAMS, p. 10; Art_Photo/Shutterstock.com, p. 11; fizkes/Shutterstock.com, p. 12; Monkey Business Images/Shutterstock.com, pp. 13, 27; Geber86/E+/Getty Images, p. 14; jsmith/E+/Getty Images, p. 15; wutzkohphoto/Shutterstock.com, p. 16; Aleksandar Malivuk/Shutterstock.com, p. 17; karelnoppe/Shutterstock.com, p. 18; Koltsov/Shutterstock.com, p. 19; FamVeld/Shutterstock.com, pp. 20, 21; Denis Kuvaev/Shutterstock.com, p. 22; ArtMarie/E+/Getty Images, p. 23; Marharyta Gangalo/Shutterstock.com, p. 24; Dragon Images/Shutterstock.com, p. 26.

Lerner Publications Company
An imprint of Lerner Publishing Group, Inc.
241 First Avenue North
Minneapolis, MN 55401 USA

For reading levels and more information, look up this title at www.lernerbooks.com.

Main body text set in Mikado Medium.
Typeface provided by HVD Fonts.

Editor: Alison Lorenz **Designer:** Emily Harris
Lerner team: Martha Kranes

Library of Congress Cataloging-in-Publication Data

Names: Lindeen, Mary, author.
Title: Stay healthy with Sesame Street : understanding coronavirus / Mary Lindeen.
Description: Minneapolis : Lerner Publications, 2021 | Includes bibliographical references and index. | Audience: Ages 4–8 | Audience: Grades K–1 | Summary: "Familiar characters from Sesame Street and a friendly question-and-answer format help make the subjects of coronavirus, COVID-19, physical distancing, and quarantine accessible to young children"— Provided by publisher.
Identifiers: LCCN 2020028311 (print) | LCCN 2020028312 (ebook) | ISBN 9781728427621 (library binding) | ISBN 9781728427645 (ebook)
Subjects: LCSH: COVID-19 (Disease) | Children—Miscellanea.
Classification: LCC RA644.C67 L56 2021 (print) | LCC RA644.C67 (ebook) | DDC 616.2/4140083—dc23

LC record available at https://lccn.loc.gov/2020028311
LC ebook record available at https://lccn.loc.gov/2020028312

Manufactured in the United States of America
2-50295-49445-2/18/2021